Grayslake Area Public Library District
Grayslake, Illinois

1. A fine will be charged on each book which is not returned when it is due.

2. All injuries to books beyond reasonable wear and all losses shall be made good to the satisfaction of the Librarian.

3. Each borrower is held responsible for all books drawn on his card and for all fines accruing on the same.

DEMCO

A Note to Parents

DK READERS is a compelling program for beginning readers, designed in conjunction with leading literacy experts, including Dr. Linda Gambrell, Professor of Education at Clemson University. Dr. Gambrell has served as President of the National Reading Conference, the College Reading Association, and the International Reading Association.

Beautiful illustrations and superb full-color photographs combine with engaging, easy-to-read stories to offer a fresh approach to each subject in the series. Each DK READER is guaranteed to capture a child's interest while developing his or her reading skills, general knowledge, and love of reading.

The five levels of DK READERS are aimed at different reading abilities, enabling you to choose the books that are exactly right for your child:

Pre-level 1: Learning to read
Level 1: Beginning to read
Level 2: Beginning to read alone
Level 3: Reading alone
Level 4: Proficient readers

The "normal" age at which a child begins to read can be anywhere from three to eight years old. Adult participation through the lower levels is very helpful for providing encouragement, discussing storylines, and sounding out unfamiliar words.

No matter which level you select, you can be sure that you are helping your child learn to read, then read to learn!

LONDON, NEW YORK, MUNICH,
MELBOURNE, and DELHI

For Brady Games
Publisher David Waybright
Editor-in-Chief H. Leigh Davis
Publisher David Waybright
Licensing Director Mike Degler
Marketing Director Debby Neubauer
International Translations Brian Saliba
Title Manager Tim Fitzpatrick

For DK Publishing
Publishing Director Beth Sutinis
Reading Consultant
Linda Gambrell, Ph.D.

Produced by
Shoreline Publishing Group LLC
President James Buckley Jr.
Designer Tom Carling, carlingdesign.com

DK/BradyGAMES
800 East 96th St., 3rd floor
Indianapolis, IN 46240

09 10 11 10 9 8 7 6 5 4 3 2

A catalog record for this book is available from the Library of Congress.

ISBN: 978-0-7566-4433-8 (Paperback)
ISBN: 978-0-7566-4478-9 (Hardback)

Printed and bound by Lake Book.

Discover more at
www.dk.com

Contents

DK READERS

Explore with
Ash and Dawn

Written by Michael Teitelbaum

DK

DK Publishing

Welcome to Pokémon

So you want to learn about the Pokémon world, but you're not sure where to start? No problem. Two great friends, Ash and Dawn, are here to help you explore the amazing world of Pokémon.

These great Trainers will help you discover some of the regions in the Pokémon world. They'll tell you about the many cities in each of those regions. You'll learn about Pokémon Centers, Pokémon Gyms, Pokémon Gym Leaders, how to earn badges, and so much more.

Pokémon Trainers

A Pokémon Trainer uses a Poké Ball to catch Pokémon. The Trainer then takes care of his or her Pokémon to keep it healthy. Trainers also help Pokémon to improve their skills in battle.

Along the way, you'll meet some of the many amazing Pokémon that these Trainers have met in their travels. Read about some of their greatest battles and find out how they used their wits to win!

So what are you waiting for? Ash and Dawn can't wait to meet you! Your tour begins right now! They choose you!

Ash with Pikachu

Meet Ash and Dawn

Say hello to Ash Ketchum. He's here with his good friend and Pokémon Coordinator, Dawn. They're here to take you on a tour of their awesome Pokémon world.

Later on, they'll show you around Dawn's home, the Sinnoh region. Right now, they'd like to welcome you to Ash's home region of Kanto.

What are all these regions? It's a good thing you asked. The Pokémon world is divided into regions. Every region has lots of cities in it. And in some of the bigger cities you can find Pokémon Gyms.

Every gym is run by a Gym Leader. All these Gym Leaders are expert Pokémon Trainers.

Pokémon Gyms

A Pokémon Gym is where Pokémon Trainers go to train their Pokémon. It's also a place where your Pokémon can battle against the Pokémon of other Trainers.

Fuchsia City Gym

A Pokémon Center

Every Pokémon Trainer hopes to
one day become a Pokémon Champion.
That was Ash's goal the day he got his
famous Pokémon, Pikachu.

The first step in becoming a Pokémon
Champion is to earn all eight badges
in a region. To earn a badge, you must
beat the Gym Leader in his or her own

gym. They are all very good. Beating them is no easy job!

Many cities also have Pokémon Centers. These are like hospitals where sick, injured, or just plain tired Pokémon come to rest and recover. Ash's friend, Nurse Joy, runs the Viridian City Pokémon Center. She helped Pikachu there when it got injured.

We promised you a tour of the Kanto region, so here we go. First stop: Pallet Town, Ash's hometown!

Nurse Joy

There are actually many Nurse Joys in the various regions of the Pokémon world. They all work at Pokémon Centers helping to heal sick or injured Pokémon.

The Kanto Region

It seems like only yesterday that Ash was in Professor Oak's lab in Pallet Town to get his Pokémon. Beginning Pokémon Trainers in the Kanto region go there to get their first Pokémon. New Trainers in Kanto can choose a Bulbasaur, a Charmander, or a Squirtle.

We know what you're thinking—how did Ash end up with Pikachu? The truth is, he overslept on the day he was supposed to get his first Pokémon! By the time he got to Professor Oak's lab, the other three Pokémon were already taken. Pikachu was the last Pokémon that Professor Oak had left to give Ash.

Boy, we sure are glad Ash overslept that day. We can't imagine Ash without his buddy Pikachu!

Brock, Ash, and Misty

Ash set out from Pallet Town to begin his quest to become the world's greatest Pokémon Champion. Along the way Ash made some new friends, like Misty, Brock, and Tracey Sketchit. As Ash traveled, he also caught lots of Pokémon, like Bulbasaur, Charmander, Caterpie, and Snorlax.

In Viridian City Ash saw his first Pokémon Center and his first Poké Mart. A Poké Mart is where Trainers can get supplies for their Pokémon. Some of the cool things you'll find in a Poké Mart include an Awakening item in case your Pokémon falls asleep. You can get Burn Heal to soothe burns if your Pokémon battles a Fire-type Pokémon. There's also Ice Heal, to defrost your frozen Pokémon after a battle with an Ice-type Pokémon.

A good Trainer always knows what he or she needs to take care of his or her Pokémon—and where to get it!

Charmander

Our tour
continues near
Viridian City,
in the Viridian
Forest. This place
is filled with Bug-
type Pokémon. This is
where Ash caught his first
wild Pokémon: Caterpie, a
Bug-type Pokémon, naturally!

Caterpie

Here in Pewter City, north of the
forest, Ash met his first Gym Leader,
Brock. He thought he'd win
his first badge against
Brock. But Pikachu was no
match for Brock's Rock-type
Pokémon, Geodude and Onix.
Pikachu used attacks like
Thundershock and Thunderbolt.

But the rock-hard Geodude was not affected. Meanwhile, Onix is a long and powerful Rock-type that likes to live underground. Together, they were able to defeat Ash and his Pokémon. Oh, well! He can try again some time!

Moving on in our tour, next we'll visit the caves of Mt. Moon. Be careful. Watch out for the Zubat! This is where Ash saw a Clefairy carrying a Moon Stone. Legends say that the Moon Stone increases a Pokémon's power.

Geodude

Pokédex

Ash's friend Professor Oak invented the Pokédex. The Pokédex is a handheld electronic encyclopedia with information about all the different Pokémon.

A Pokédex from Sinnoh

Next we move to Cerulean City, where Ash's friend Misty lives. She and her sisters are the Gym Leaders here. If you love Water-type Pokémon like Staryu, then Cerulean City is the place for you.

Another place in Kanto is Vermillion City. It is the only city in the Kanto region with a port. Ash even ended up taking a cruise on a big ship called the *St. Anne*. On board, Ash's Butterfree fought a tough battle against a Raticate.

The last stop on our tour of the exciting Kanto region is Saffron City. It's the biggest city in all of the Kanto region. It is so big, there are two Pokémon Gyms here. The Silph Company is also here in Saffron City. They make Poké Balls and other stuff you'll find in a Poké Mart.

Of course, Kanto region is so big we can't possibly see it all. But no tour of the region would be complete without a look at its Pokémon Gyms.

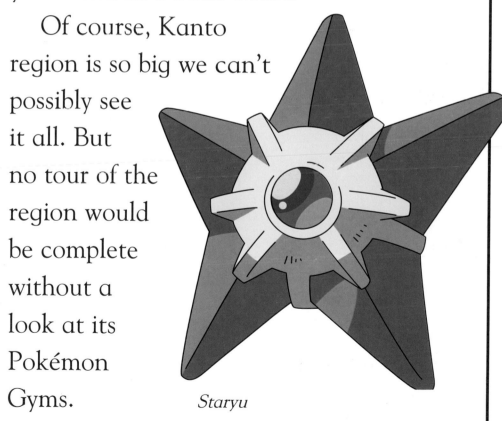

Staryu

Kanto's Pokémon Gyms

In order to earn all eight badges in the Pokémon Gyms located in the Kanto region, Ash had to battle some pretty good Gym Leaders. Fortunately, his Pokémon were up to the task.

Although he lost to the Pewter City Gym Leader, Brock, on his first visit there, in time, he did earn his badge. For beating Brock and his Rock-type Pokémon in their second battle,

Brock

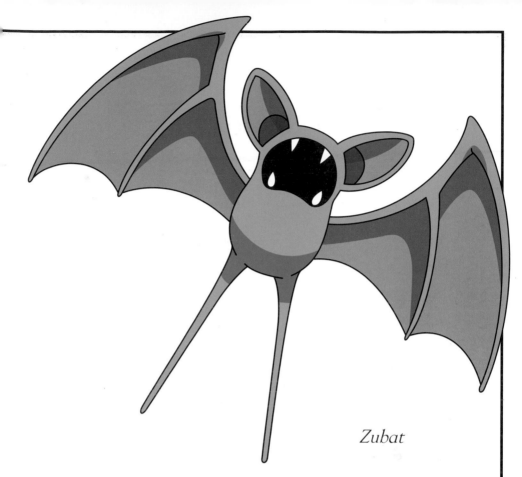

Zubat

he earned the Boulder Badge. Even
though Brock is a great Gym Leader,
what he really loves to do is to care
for his Pokémon. He wants to be a
Breeder. He likes this even more than
entering battles. And so Brock joined
Ash and Misty on their journey to
catch Pokémon and see new places.

After being friends with Misty for a while, Ash finally got to visit her home, Cerulean City. She and her sisters are the Gym Leaders there. They specialize in training Water-type Pokémon. Misty's Goldeen and Starmie are her favorites in the gym. That's where Ash earned his Cascade Badge. Misty left the Gym Leader duties to her sisters and joined him on his journey through the Kanto region.

At the Vermillion City Gym, Ash battled Gym Leader Lt. Surge. He's a big, tough guy, and he's kind of scary looking!

Starmie

Misty, Pikachu, and Ash

But here's the thing about him: he thinks that winning battles is more important than caring for his Pokémon. He evolves his Pokémon too quickly, before they learn all they need to know. Because of that, Pikachu was able to beat Lt. Surge's Raichu and Ash earned his Thunder Badge.

Alakazam

Maybe the most unusual Gym Leader Ash ever met was Sabrina. She runs the Saffron City Gym. And, get this—she has psychic powers! So what do you think her favorite type of Pokémon are?

You guessed it—Psychic-type Pokémon, like Kadabra and Alakazam. Ash had to travel to a tower in Lavender City to find a Ghost-type Pokémon in order to beat her and earn his Marsh Badge.

At the Celadon City Gym Ash met Erika, the Gym Leader there. She loves nature and gardening, so naturally she loves Grass-type Pokémon.

During his battle with Erika, Team Rocket started a fire in her gym. They're always causing trouble! When Ash rescued Erika's Gloom, she thanked him by giving him a Rainbow Badge. Awesome!

Gloom

Koga, the Gym Leader at the Fuchsia City Gym, is a ninja master. His fighting strategy is to use tricks rather than strength. And his gym is in a cool old mansion. It's filled with all kinds of booby traps, like slanted rooms and invisible walls. Ash's battle with

Koga started inside the mansion. It finished outside in the courtyard. There, Ash's Charmander beat Koga's Poison-type Pokémon. Ash earned his Soul Badge.

Electric-type Voltorb occupy Koga's mansion.

At the Cinnabar Gym, Gym Leader Blaine loves Fire-type Pokémon. Maybe that's why his gym is

Blaine loves Fire-type Pokémon, like this Magmar.

inside an active volcano! He also loves
riddles. But when Ash's Charizard beat
his Magmar using a Seismic Toss, he
earned a Volcano Badge.

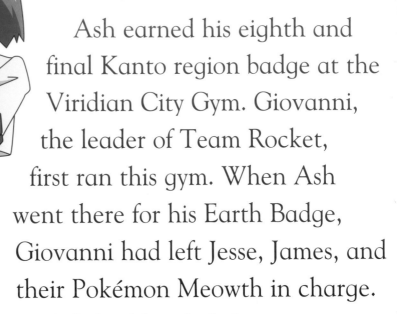

James

Ash earned his eighth and
final Kanto region badge at the
Viridian City Gym. Giovanni,
the leader of Team Rocket,
first ran this gym. When Ash
went there for his Earth Badge,
Giovanni had left Jesse, James, and
their Pokémon Meowth in charge.
Ash had battled this trio many
times. They always gave him
trouble, but he knew he had to take
them on. They stood between him
and his final badge from the
Kanto region.

Team Rocket Wants Pikachu

Team Rocket is a group of
troublemakers led by Giovanni.
His agents, Jesse, James, and their
Pokémon Meowth, are always
hatching plots to steal Ash's Pikachu.

This time, they even rigged the gym to shock anyone they battled. But Ash managed to turn that against them and earned an Earth Badge.

Meowth

We could go on and on about Kanto, but we know you'd like to see other regions, too. Now that you know about Ash's home region and some of the fun he had there, we're ready to tell you all about Dawn's home region, Sinnoh. So let's get started!

Jesse

The Sinnoh Region

We hope you enjoyed learning all
about the Kanto region. Now we get to
tell you all about Dawn's home region of
Sinnoh. We're starting here in Twinleaf

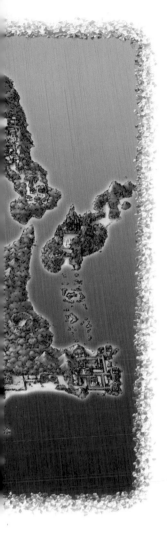

Town, her hometown. It's a beautiful, small town near a lake called Lake Verity. One of the things Dawn loves best about her hometown is that the air always smells like fresh leaves . . . Mmmm. Dawn left here to begin her Pokémon journey.

Now we're in Sandgem Town. Don't you love the salty smell of the fresh sea air? Sandgem Town has a Pokémon Center and a Poké Mart. It's also where Professor Rowan's lab is. He's the Pokémon expert of the Sinnoh region. In fact, did you know he's an old friend of Professor Oak's? He is!

Turtwig   *Piplup*

In Kanto, Professor Oak assigns the Pokémon. But here in the Sinnoh region, it's Professor Rowan who gives beginning Trainers their starting Pokémon. In Sinnoh, they choose between Piplup, Turtwig, and Chimchar.

Professor Rowan gave Dawn a Piplup, a Water-type Pokémon. But Piplup didn't always obey her at first, kind of like Ash and Pikachu. But

Chimchar

just like them, Piplup and Dawn have become great pals. Since that time Dawn has caught Buneary, Pachirisu, and Buizel. She also traded for Aipom.

Now let's move on to Jubilife City. It sure is big! In fact, Jubilife City is the biggest city in the Sinnoh region. It's got a great Poké Mart. And it's home to the Pokétech Company, maker of the Pokétech. That's a special watch that Pokémon Trainers in the Sinnoh region wear. Jubilife City is where Dawn entered her first Pokémon Contest.

Pokémon Contests among Pokémon Coordinators are held here in Sinnoh. A Coordinator is a type of Trainer who trains his or her Pokémon not just for

Zoey's Glameow defeated Dawn's Buneary.

battles, but also for Pokémon Contests. In these contests, Pokémon are judged by how they look and move as much as how they battle. The winners get a special ribbon.

Some Trainers in Sinnoh compete in contests, some battle at Pokémon Gyms. And a few do both!

At the contest in Jubilife City, Dawn used her Buneary against Zoey's Glameow. Zoey won the ribbon there, but they also became friends.

Here we are in Floaroma Town. Everything here smells like flowers.

Floaroma holds a special place in Dawn's heart because it's where she won her first Pokémon Contest. And it was Dawn's first Pokémon, Piplup, who helped her win the Floaroma Ribbon.

Hearthome City is home to the Super Contest Hall where the Super Contest is held. Isn't it a fun place? Just look at all those Pokémon, out of their Poké Balls, wandering around Amity Square. Even though Dawn lost

Like Mother, Like Daughter

Dawn's mother, Johanna, was also a Pokémon Coordinator. In fact, just before Dawn set out on her own Pokémon journey to become a coordinator, her mother gave her one of the contest ribbons she had won when she was a Pokémon Coordinator.

Dawn defeated Team Rocket's Jesse in the first round on her way to winning the Floaroma Ribbon.

in the Hearthome Super Contest, we still think the city is great.

We know you're excited to learn about the Pokémon Gyms of the Sinnoh region. Let's not wait any longer—here we go!

Sinnoh's Pokémon Gyms

Oreburgh City is home to the first Pokémon Gym in the Sinnoh region. You can also find the Oreburgh Mine there. In fact, Roark, the Gym Leader there, is also a mining foreman! If you can beat him, you'll earn a Coal Badge.

Let's next trek through the dark and mysterious Eterna Forest. It's home to lots of Bug- and Grass-type Pokémon. Then we arrive at Eterna City, home of the next Pokémon Gym. The Gym Leader there, Gardenia, is an expert in Grass-type Pokémon. She loves to use her

Cherubi, a Grass-type Pokémon

Infernape, a Fire-and-Fighting-type Pokémon

Cherubi, her Turtwig, and her Roserade in battles. But if you beat Gardenia, you'll earn the Forest Badge.

The Veilstone City Gym Leader, Maylene, uses Fighting-type Pokémon. She is an expert at choosing which of these tough Pokémon are right to fight! If you beat her, you'll get a Cobble Badge.

Drifblim, a Ghost-and-Flying-type Pokémon

On the edge of a giant swamp in the Sinnoh region called the Great Marsh, Pastoria City is the place to find Water-type Pokémon. Crasher Wake is the Gym Leader there. If you beat him, you'll earn a Fen Badge.

Even though Dawn competed in a contest in Hearthome City, she never got to meet Fantina, the Gym Leader there. She really likes Ghost-type Pokémon, like Drifblim. And if you beat Fantina in her gym, you'll take home a Relic Badge.

Remember Roark, the first Gym Leader we met with Ash? Well, Roark's father, Byron, is also a Gym Leader. He runs the Pokémon Gym in Canalave City. He uses Steel-type Pokémon, like Bronzor, Bastiodon, and Steelix. Beat his Pokémon and you'll earn the Mine Badge.

Bronzor, a Steel-and-Psychic-type Pokémon

Snowpoint City, home of the next Pokémon Gym, is named just right. It's in the far northern part of the Sinnoh region and it always seems to be cold and snowy there. It's no surprise that Candice, the Snowpoint Gym Leader, loves Ice-type Pokémon. If you beat her in this snowy world, what type of badge do you think you'll win? The Icicle Badge of course!

Raichu, the evolved form of Pikachu

Sunyshore City is the final gym we'll visit in the Sinnoh region. It's got the sea on one side and mountains on the other. Volkner, the Gym Leader here, loves Electric-type Pokémon, including Raichu, the evolved version of Pikachu. If you beat Volkner and collect a Beacon Badge, you'll complete a clean sweep of all eight gyms.

Well, we hope you liked the tour of the Sinnoh region. We can't wait for Ash to compete in all of those gyms and earn all eight badges. Being able to visit other regions and meet new Trainers and Pokémon is one of the best things about being a Pokémon Trainer!

Other Places

We sure hope you're having fun seeing all these places! That was a

great tour of the Sinnoh region. There was so much to see! But, of course, there are more than the Kanto and Sinnoh regions in the world of Pokémon. We have a feeling you might enjoy learning about the other places that Ash has visited.

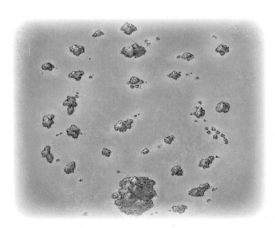

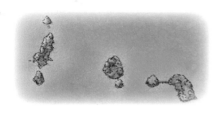 The best way to get to the Orange Islands is to fly there by blimp or by hot air balloon. You can take a boat, but it's a long, bumpy ride.

Then again, if you're a Pokémon Trainer who happens  to have a big Flying-type Pokémon, such as Pidgeot, you can always hop on its back and hitch a ride. While they aren't a region, the Orange Islands are home to Pokémon Trainers and Gyms.

Pidgeot

The Orange League in the Orange Islands includes the Gym Leaders of the Orange Crew. Trainers really like competing in that league. Here's why: It's not all about just how your Pokémon battles. What counts there is how you work with and care for your Pokémon.

That's one of the things many people like about being a Pokémon Trainer. It's all about friendship, trust, loyalty, and teamwork. That's what you need to succeed.

Prima, one of the great Orange Islands Pokémon Champions, put it the best when he said, "In the Orange League, the most important thing is that the Trainer and his or her Pokémon be of a single heart."

We couldn't have said it better!

Cissy, Danny, Rudy, and Luana, members of the Orange Crew

Chikorita

The Johto region is close to Ash's home region of Kanto. It has eight gyms of its own. A Pokémon Trainer must beat eight Gym Leaders there to earn badges and compete against the Elite Four, the four best Trainers in the region.

If you want to start out as a Pokémon Trainer in the Johto region, you have to visit Professor Elm in his lab in New Bark Town. There he starts you off with a Chikorita, a Totodile, or a Cyndaquil.

Enjoy a visit to a warm part of the world of Pokémon when you visit the Hoenn region. To be a Trainer there, you need to see Professor Birch in Littleroot Town. From there, you start with a Treecko, a Torchic, or a Mudkip. Good luck!

The Pokémon world is big. It takes years to explore it all. Thanks so much for joining us on our tour. And now, your own adventure is just beginning!

Professor Birch

Orange Crew badges

Badges and The Elite Four

Every region has its Elite Four—the four best Pokémon Trainers in the region. Once a Pokémon Trainer has earned all the badges in a region, he or she can battle the Elite Four.

Glossary

Antidote
A medicine that is given to cure being poisoned.

Badge
A pin that shows a person has achieved something special. In the world of Pokémon, a badge means you have defeated a Gym Leader.

Blimp
A balloon-like airship.

Booby Trap
A trick set up to catch something by surprise.

Courtyard
A large, open area outside a house.

Cruise
A journey by boat.

Encyclopedia
A book filled with information.

Evolve
Develop or change. In the Pokémon world, it's when a Pokémon changes into its next form.

Goal
Something you hope to achieve.

Lab
A place where a scientist does research or conducts experiments.

Mansion
A big, fancy house.

Ninja
A special kind of martial arts warrior.

Obey
To do what you are told.

Potion
A liquid that has magical or medicinal qualities.

Psychic
Special mental powers to read minds or predict the future.

Quest
A journey to accomplish something.

Region
An area or section of a country or world.

Responsibilities
Jobs a person must do.

Rival
Opponent, someone you compete against.

Trek
Walk or hike.

Trio
Three of something.

Index